Stage Kiss

———————

Stage Kiss

Sarah Ruhl

THEATRE COMMUNICATIONS GROUP
NEW YORK
2014

Stage Kiss is published by Theatre Communications Group, Inc., 520 Eighth Avenue, 24th Floor, New York, NY 10018-4156

"The Sublime and the Good," by Iris Murdoch, *Chicago Review*: Volume 13, Number 3 (Autumn 1959), pp. 42–55.

"Some Enchanted Evening," By Richard Rodgers and Oscar Hammerstein II, copyright © 1949 by Williamson Music (ASCAP), an Imagem Company, owner of publication and allied rights throughout the world. Copyright renewed. International copyright secured. All rights reserved. Used by permission.

The publication of *Stage Kiss* by Sarah Ruhl, through TCG's Book Program, is made possible in part by the New York State Council on the Arts with the support of Governor Andrew Cuomo and the New York State Legislature.

TCG books are exclusively distributed to the book trade by Consortium Book Sales and Distribution.

LIBRARY OF CONGRESS CATALOGING-IN-PUBLICATION DATA
Ruhl, Sarah, 1974–
Stage Kiss / Sarah Ruhl.
pages cm
ISBN 978-1-55936-470-6 (paperback)
ISBN 978-1-55936-429-4 (ebook)
I. Title.
PS3618.U48S73   2014
812'.6—dc23   2014019184

Book design and composition by Lisa Govan
Cover design by Rodrigo Corral Design / Rachel Adam Rogers

First Edition, December 2014
Third Printing, January 2024

For actors
For first loves
But most of all, for my husband

———————————————

Stage Kiss

Production History

Stage Kiss had its world premiere at the Goodman Theatre (Robert Falls, Artistic Director; Roche Schulfer, Executive Director) in Chicago on May 9, 2011. It was directed by Jessica Thebus. The set design was by Todd Rosenthal, the costume design was by Linda Roethke, the lighting design was by James F. Ingalls, the sound design was by Andre J. Pluess; the dramaturg was Neena Arndt, the fight choreographer was Nick Sandys and the production stage manager was Joseph Drummond. The cast was:

SHE	Jenny Bacon
HE	Mark L. Montgomery
DIRECTOR	Ross Lehman
KEVIN/BUTLER/DOCTOR/PIMP	Jeffrey Carlson
HUSBAND/HARRISON	Scott Jaeck
ANGELA/MAID/MILLIE	Sarah Tolan-Mee
MILLICENT/LAURIE	Erica Elam

Stage Kiss had its New York premiere at Playwrights Horizons (Tim Sanford, Artistic Director; Leslie Marcus, Managing Director) on March 2, 2014. It was directed by Rebecca Taichman. The set design was by Neil Patel, the costume design was by Susan Hilferty, the lighting design was by Peter Kaczorowski, the sound design was by Matt Hubbs, the original music was by Todd Almond; the choreographer was Sam Pinkleton, the fight choreographer was Turner Smith and the production stage manager was Cole P. Bonenberger. The cast was:

SHE	Jessica Hecht
HE	Dominic Fumusa
DIRECTOR	Patrick Kerr
KEVIN/BUTLER/DOCTOR/PIMP	Michael Cyril Creighton
HUSBAND/HARRISON	Daniel Jenkins
ANGELA/MAID/MILLIE	Emma Galvin
MILLICENT/LAURIE	Clea Alsip
THE ACCOMPANIST	Todd Almond

Characters

1. A woman—She—in her mid-forties. Plays the role of Ada Wilcox.
2. A man—He—in his mid-forties. Plays the role of Johnny Lowell.
3. A director, Adrian Schwalbach.
4. Kevin, the reader. Also plays the understudy, the doctor, the butler and the pimp.
5. The husband, or Harrison.
6. Millie and the maid in Act One; Angela in Act Two. An actress in her early twenties who can believably play a teenager.
7. Millicent in Act One; Laurie in Act Two. An actress in her late twenties or early thirties.

Set

The set has three modes which should easily transform.
A red curtain would be nice to set off the plays within plays.

1. A raw theater space (emptiness, the thing itself).
2. A 1930s stage set (artifice happy to be artifice; think: gorgeous painted drops and flats).
3. A naturalistically messy East Village apartment, as real as possible (artifice ashamed of its own artifice; think: an installation).

Love is the extremely difficult realization that something other than oneself is real.

—*Iris Murdoch*

Act One

Scene 1—Audition

Lights up on a raw, empty theater space.
Chairs.
A piano.

SHE

Sorry the train was—I'm so late—I'm so sorry—
Do you still want me to—?

DIRECTOR

No problem.

SHE

Great. Okay. Is this—?

DIRECTOR

Yes, Kevin will be reading with you.

SHE

Nice to meet you, Kevin. Do you want me to actually kiss Kevin, or Kevin do you mind if we kiss; you look young, I don't want to traumatize you.

KEVIN

No—please, go ahead.

SHE

Could you position your chair this way then? Sorry, is that weird? I had sort of pictured your chair this way. Should I start?

DIRECTOR

Whenever you're ready.

SHE

Okay. I'll start then. Wait, I'll just move my chair. Is that all right?

DIRECTOR

Great.

A pause.

SHE

Sorry—can I ask one thing?

DIRECTOR

Of course.

SHE

I just got the sides because my agent blah blah blah and I didn't have time to read the whole thing, so do you mind just telling me the plot a little bit because I only have these four pages—

During the following, She vocalizes some responses—ums and ohs—that register her narrative empathy and interest.

DIRECTOR

Sure. You're told in the first scene that you have a month to live. You have a rare degenerative disorder. And you say to yourself: I need to see my old love before I die. And you cable him and he comes for a visit, he lives in Sweden, so he stays with you for a month, in your penthouse in Manhattan. It's a very nice apartment as your husband is a very wealthy train mogul. You and your first love pick up right where you left off, but your husband is so noble that he doesn't object. And seeing your old love has reversed your disease and you are becoming healthier and healthier. In the third act your daughter comes home from Paris and your first love falls in love with your daughter, and takes her to Sweden. So you are left alone, to pick up the pieces.

And there are some really very funny bits in the middle when you're all living together under one roof but some really sort of sad bits, you know, when you're ill, and the generosity of your husband in letting your old lover stay with you. Which I find very moving. So it's tonally, very you know, slippery. And it was a flop on Broadway in 1932 but we think with the proper cast, a new score, and some judicious cuts it will be really very well received in New Haven.

SHE

Got it.

DIRECTOR

What else . . . there are one or two musical numbers. You do sing, don't you?

SHE

Oh—yes.

DIRECTOR

So, have a go?

SHE

(To Kevin) Are you playing the husband *and* the lover?

11

Kevin nods.

SHE

All, right so I'll just pretend the husband is here *(Pointing in another direction, away from Kevin)* and you're there. *(Pointing to Kevin)*

KEVIN

Okay.

SHE AS ADA

(Looking at an imaginary person off to the side) I can't bear cocktails anymore, I'm afraid.

KEVIN AS HUSBAND

Water then?

SHE AS ADA

Yes.

KEVIN AS HUSBAND

In the solarium or in the study?

SHE AS ADA

The study I think. Have Jenkins put everything out.

The imaginary husband exits in the play, but of course, Kevin just sits.

SHE

(To Kevin) He just exited right?

KEVIN

Right.

She follows the imaginary husband out with her eyes and turns back to Kevin, with passion.

SHE AS ADA

(To Kevin, as the lover) God, I love you. I love you I love you
I love you.

They kiss.

SHE AS ADA

Your lips taste like—let me taste them again.

She kisses him again.

SHE AS ADA

Of cherries? No.

KEVIN

I'm so sorry, I'm so sweaty, the elevator's broken—

SHE

Oh no, you're beautiful.

She kisses him again.

SHE AS ADA

Of chestnuts.
Oh, God, I want to kiss you all day!

KEVIN AS LOVER

And I you.

She kisses him again. She starts laughing.

SHE

Sorry—there was a little crumb in your mouth.

KEVIN

Oh, sorry.

He wipes the crumb.

DIRECTOR

Should we take it from the top? You don't have to kiss this time, you could just indicate the kissing—with a gesture of some kind.

SHE

A gesture?

DIRECTOR

Sure.

SHE

Okay. Fine.

SHE AS ADA

(Turning toward Kevin as the lover) God, I love you. I love you I love you I love you.

She sits on Kevin's lap and makes a strange gesture substituting for the kiss.

SHE AS ADA

Your lips taste like—let me taste them again.

Strange kiss gesture, still sitting on his lap.

SHE AS ADA

Of cherries? No.

Strange gesture, still sitting on his lap.

SHE AS ADA

Of chestnuts.
Oh, God, I want to kiss you all day!

KEVIN AS LOVER

And I you—

SHE AS ADA

(Overlapping with "And I you") Until I am breathless with desire. The way I was when I was eighteen. Do you remember the lake?

KEVIN AS LOVER

I think I hear your husband.

SHE AS ADA

Hang it all!

KEVIN AS LOVER

Oh, darling. How can we have been apart this long?

SHE AS ADA

I do not know.
I do not know.

She stops and looks at the director. A pause.

DIRECTOR

Very nice work.

SHE

Oh, thank you.
Really?

DIRECTOR

Yes.

SHE

Do you want me to do the second side?

DIRECTOR

No, that won't be necessary.

SHE

I memorized it.

DIRECTOR

If you'd like to, go ahead.

SHE

Do you want to tell me anything about it?

DIRECTOR

Just have a go.

She fumbles with her papers.

SHE

All right.
I think I'll stand, is it all right if I stand?

DIRECTOR

Whatever makes you most comfortable.

SHE

I'll stand. No, I'll sit.

She sits.

DIRECTOR

Great.

SHE

(To Kevin) So now—you'll be Millicent?

KEVIN

Right.

SHE AS ADA

Millicent, I've realized the reason it was impossible, so long
ago . . .

KEVIN AS MILLICENT

There is always a reason, isn't there?

SHE AS ADA

He was like champagne, *champagne*, but you can't live on champagne your whole life, eventually you want bread, my husband is like bread—oh the smell of toast in the morning!

KEVIN AS MILLICENT

You think Jack is like—toast?

SHE AS ADA

But like the best toast in the world, no crumbs, *(Seeing Kevin, laughing, then recovering)* sorry, a toast that feeds you and feeds you in winter and is spread with the most gorgeous butter . . . I used to be afraid of putting too much butter on my toast, but the first night I spent with Jack, I woke up in the morning, and he put enormous quantities of butter on my toast, and I thought: I'll love this man forever.

KEVIN AS MILLICENT

It's such a relief to love your husband, is it not?

SHE AS ADA

(Saying the word "clear" the same way three times) Yes! Millicent, do you think that if life were properly understood, it would be beautiful all the time? Clear, clear, clear!
(As herself) Sorry, can I go back?

DIRECTOR

Sure.

SHE AS ADA

(Saying the word "clear" differently every time) Millicent, do you think that if life were properly understood, it would be beautiful all the time? Clear, clear clear?

KEVIN AS MILLICENT

I think your life is beautiful, darling Ada . . . don't leave us . . . don't leave—me . . .

SHE AS ADA

I shan't . . . I feel myself coming into the world again, I feel my strength returning. Millicent, I want to live. And I will live. (*As herself*) This is where I sing?

DIRECTOR

Yes.

Either we have an accompanist who nods to her and starts playing, or else she says:

SHE

A capella?

And the director nods.
She sings:

SHE AS ADA

Love me just shy of forever
Or love me till six o clock
Love me whatever the weather
Love me in afghan or sweater
Whether it's May or December
Oh love me just shy of forever
Darling
Love me past six o clock.

She stops singing and looks at the director.

SHE

Was that all right?
That was awful, I know, I can learn to sing, and I can learn to act, ha ha . . .
Good-bye.

She exits, quickly.
Kevin and the director look at each other.
She comes back.

SHE

I think I just left my bag . . .

She grabs her bag, everything topples out of it.

SHE

Oh, right, the minor humiliations of life . . . sorry . . . good luck with your day, hope you see some good people, I haven't auditioned for a play in like ten years . . .

Everything keeps toppling out of her bag: water bottle, script, hairbrush, lipstick, etc.

SHE

Oh, just shoot me now . . . ha ha ha . . . Bye, *(To director)* thank you, *(To Kevin)* bye Tom—Devin—

KEVIN

Kevin—

SHE

Kevin!—you were great, I hope I didn't get lipstick on you, I got this lipstick as a free sample you know and I think it was the wrong color for the character, it's called Desert Storm, no that's a war, Desert Flower, wouldn't you love to have the job of naming lipsticks—or wars . . . right, okay, then, shoot me now. Okay, thanks guys, have a good afternoon.

She exits.
The reader and the director look at each other.

DIRECTOR

(With optimism and sincerity) She was good.

Scene 2

The first rehearsal.

> HE

Hello.

> SHE

Hello.

> HE

I didn't think you were working these days.

> SHE

I wasn't. I had a child.

> HE

I'd heard. How old?

> SHE

Sixteen.

HE

That's great.

SHE

Great?

HE

Great.

SHE

Great is such a—word. You didn't have them—

HE

Words—

SHE	HE
Children.	No.

SHE

Of course I know that. We did at least have two friends in common. Not many but enough to know whether you procreated. Not that I was keeping track. But you run into people. Occasionally.

HE

Right.

SHE

But of our two friends, one of them is now dead and the other's in Berlin.

HE

Right.
Sad about—

SHE

Wasn't it? I didn't see you at the funeral.

HE

I sent flowers.

SHE

That was thoughtful. I mean given that you couldn't come, or didn't make the effort to come, it was nice you sent flowers. They were—pungent. As I remember.

HE

Mm.
You didn't know I was—going to be in the play?

SHE

No. I didn't ask. I haven't worked—for a while. When they called, I said: yes. I didn't ask: can I have approval over who's playing my lover in New Haven? If you are an actress in this country you are either Juliet or Lady Macbeth and there's nothing in between . . . So I think in the last ten years I've had two auditions, one for a maid on Broadway and one for an antidepressant commercial. I got the antidepressant commercial.

HE

Yeah, I saw it.
You were good.

SHE

Sure.

HE

I mean—you seemed depressed—and then you seemed happy.

SHE

Right.
So you didn't know that I—

HE

No.
Are they playing some kind of fucking joke on us?

SHE

No one cares who I fucked during puberty. No one even wonders.

HE

It wasn't exactly puberty.

SHE

Emotional puberty, maybe.

Enter the director, holding flowers, hearing the last two lines.

DIRECTOR

Right. You two know each other?

They nod.

SHE

Mmm.

DIRECTOR

Great. That'll make things easier.

They all look at each other.

SHE

Flowers?

DIRECTOR

From your husband.

SHE

Oh! He remembered!

HE

Roses.

SHE

I like the small ones. I don't like the big ones.

HE

I know.

The company enters.

DIRECTOR

Right. Welcome, welcome. Okay. I hate sitting around a table on the first day of rehearsal. This is the theater, after all! Why hide behind a table! Let's just get on our feet immediately. Should we take it from the butler's entrance?

SHE

Uh, can I have a script?

DIRECTOR

Oh sorry sorry. YES.

The director goes to get a script.

HE

My girlfriend won't be overly pleased about this.

SHE

You have a girlfriend?

HE

Yes.

SHE

Are you in love?

HE

She's a schoolteacher. She's nice. So it probably won't work out.

SHE

You could be nicer.

HE

You could mind your own fucking business.

SHE

Yes. Well. She could be meaner.

24

HE

That's right. She could. That would be helpful, actually.

Suddenly a butler (Kevin) enters their conversation.
The director enters with She's script.

KEVIN AS BUTLER

One whiskey sour for you, sir.

SHE

Sorry—page number?

HE

Seven—
(As Johnny, holding script) Why, thank you, Jenkins.

KEVIN

And then I exit? Is there a door?

DIRECTOR

Stage right.

The butler exits.

SHE AS ADA

(Script in hand) Get out! Get out before I kick you out!

HE AS JOHNNY

Ada, darling!

SHE

The telephone rings.
You want me to mime it?

DIRECTOR

For now.

Picking up the pretend telephone.

25

SHE AS ADA

Yes, Millicent, the old cad is right here with me in fact.

She hangs up.

SHE AS ADA

Hide.

HE AS JOHNNY

No thanks! I don't mind hiding in a bedroom but hiding in a library seems kind of dry.

A pause. They stand there.

SHE

Hide.

HE

(To her) So . . . where do you want me to hide?

They look at the director.

DIRECTOR

I realize that if we're really going to do this you'll need to feel located. We need to spike the furniture. Take ten! Duct tape! Where is the duct tape?! Where is the stage manager?!

She and He both pull out their cell phones.
He and She look at each other.
They look away.
Music and lights.
They look at each other.

SHE	HE
I've dreamed of you most nights for the last twenty years. I dream I introduce you to my child.	I've dreamed of you most nights for the last twenty years.

SHE	HE
	I dream you want to kill me and that you're trying to climb through my windows. I'm
I dream that you introduce me to your lover and I clasp her hand and I like her.	frightened.
	I dream that you introduce me to your lover and I hate him.
And then I kill her.	
	I dream that you're married.
I dream that you're dead.	
	I dream that you introduce me to your child and she looks like me and we play quietly by the sea.
I dream that you teach me how to play an instrument and it is calm.	
I dream that I steal your quilt, your childhood quilt. And it's a terrible act of betrayal.	I dream that I steal your quilt, your childhood quilt. And it's a terrible act of betrayal.

Lights back to normal. They stare at each other.
Nothing was really spoken just now.

DIRECTOR
We're back. We're out of duct tape. So . . .
Here's the divan, there's the grandfather clock, there's the bal-
cony. Right.

HE
Where do you want me to hide?

DIRECTOR
Where do you feel like hiding?

27

HE

Wherever you want me to hide.

DIRECTOR

How about here. Behind the divan.

HE

Okay.

He hides behind an imaginary divan.
The husband enters, holding a script.

HUSBAND

Ada.

SHE AS ADA

Darling.

HUSBAND

The butler's having a terrible row with the parlor maid.

SHE AS ADA

Oh, bother.

HUSBAND

Is Mrs. Sternhaven coming this evening?

SHE AS ADA

No. I told her I was too ill. Be a love and be sure the flowers are
out in the entry hall, will you?

HUSBAND

Yes, my love.

She kisses him on the cheek.
The husband exits.
Then He pops out from behind the couch.

SHE AS ADA

You must leave.

HE AS JOHNNY

Oh, to hell with that! To hell with the past and the future!

They stand looking at each other and at their scripts.

DIRECTOR

And then you kiss.

HE/SHE

Right.

SHE

Today?

DIRECTOR

I like to get it out of the way—demystify it, you know.

HE

Uh—okay.
Where would you like that to happen?

DIRECTOR

What do you feel? Follow your instincts. The actor's first instincts are gold. Gold.

They look at each other.

| **SHE** | **HE** |
| Floor? | Grandfather clock? |

DIRECTOR

Let's try the balcony. Take it from: "Oh, to hell with that!"

HE AS JOHNNY

Oh, to hell with that! Kiss me.

HE

I don't see how I get her to the balcony.
I could try a sort of . . .

He awkwardly moves her to the balcony.

SHE

I don't see why he's moving me, I could just as well move him.
Like this.

She moves him to the balcony.

HE

That feels awkward.

DIRECTOR

Why don't you just stay on the divan.

HE/SHE

Fine.

DIRECTOR

Take it from . . . "Oh, to hell with that!"

HE AS JOHNNY

Oh, to hell with that! To hell with the past and the future!

They face each other.
They kiss, barely.

SHE

(To him under her breath) That was hostile.

HE

What?

SHE

(To him) Did you brush your teeth this morning?
(To the director) It's weird on the divan.

He finds a mint, perhaps on the piano, and puts it in his mouth.
She looks at him.

SHE

What if the fight is by the grandfather clock, and then we sort
of do like this, and then the kiss ends up being by the window?

DIRECTOR

Try it.

SHE AS ADA

You must leave!

HE AS JOHNNY

To hell with the past and the future! To hell with all that!

They kiss.

SHE

I think it's more of a—

They do another kind of kiss.

HE

Or I could sort of—

They do another kind of kiss.

SHE

There's no transition into the kiss, what if I, I don't know, slap
him first?

DIRECTOR

Try it.

HE AS JOHNNY

To hell with the past and the future! To hell with all that!

She slaps him.
They kiss.
They look at the director expectantly.

DIRECTOR

I—uh—

SHE

(To him, as in: Did I hit you too hard?) Was that okay?

She slaps him again.
They do another kind of kiss.
This time a memory of their old life together enters the kiss.

SHE

(To the director) Which one did you like best?

DIRECTOR

Oh, I liked them all, I just—how did you feel?

SHE
I liked the first one best.

HE
I preferred the second.

DIRECTOR

Why don't we sort of—bracket this—and move on to the next
scene? The one where you tell your daughter you're dying?

SHE
Yes.

HE
Great!

DIRECTOR

Sorry. First I'm going to pee. Five minutes everyone.

The director exits.

HE

Do you still smoke?

SHE

No. You?

HE

No.

SHE

No one smokes.

Pause.

HE

There's nothing to do on break without smoking.
I could use a cigarette.
Someone in the cast must smoke.
(Yelling) Does anyone smoke?

SHE

No one smokes.

HE

You used to roll your own. As I remember.

SHE

Did I? I can't remember.

They look at each other.
A pause.

HE

(Yelling to the cast) Does no one here smoke??

The director enters with the actress playing the daughter.

DIRECTOR

No, no one smokes. This is not the seventies.
(Gesturing to the daughter) Have you met?

SHE

You look like my daughter.

YOUNG ACTRESS

I'm actually twenty-three. People always cast me as like teenagers. It's so annoying.

SHE

Mmm.

DIRECTOR

Let's take it from: "Millie, your father and I want to have a chat."

SHE AS ADA

Millie, your father and I want to have a chat.

MILLIE

What is it, Mummy?

SHE AS ADA

Well, dear—the thing is—

HUSBAND

Your mother is—

MILLIE

I'm a big girl, Daddy. You can tell me.

Enter Johnny Lowell.

HE AS JOHNNY

Could it be—?

SHE AS ADA

Yes. This is my daughter.

HE AS JOHNNY

But you're the picture of your mother at seventeen!

SHE AS ADA

Darling, this is Johnny Lowell.

MILLIE

The famous sculptor?

SHE AS ADA

That's right.

Millie squeals.

SHE AS ADA

I didn't know you followed—sculpting.

MILLIE

Mother, I'm just back from Paris, everyone is talking about Johnny Lowell. But what were you saying about Mother?

HUSBAND

Nothing, darling. Why don't you run along and—say, Johnny, could you do us a favor and take Millie out for the afternoon?

HE AS JOHNNY

Be glad to. What say we grab a hot dog from a street vendor and swing by the Met?

MILLIE

Oh hooray! I haven't had a hot dog since I was about seven.

HUSBAND

(Handing him money for the afternoon) Thanks, Johnny.

HE AS JOHNNY

Wouldn't hear of it, old man.

Johnny and Millie exit.

DIRECTOR

(Looking at She) The tone is really slippery, isn't it. Hmm.

SHE

Are you looking at me when you say Hmm?

DIRECTOR

No, no, I'm just saying, Hmm.

SHE

Because I mean like vocally do you want me to do that weird mid-Atlantic thing, like: "I caaan't bear cocktails," I should be saying "caaan't," right, or "cuuuhnt"? But does that sound like— *(Thinking the word cunt)*

DIRECTOR

Uhh—

SHE

Or it could be more English like: "I can't bear cocktails."

DIRECTOR

Hmm.

SHE

You hate what I'm doing.

DIRECTOR

No, no.

Awkward moment.

YOUNG ACTRESS

I think I have a wig fitting.
Do I have a wig fitting?

DIRECTOR

That's right. Everyone has wig fittings. Let's stop for the day. Thanks everyone. I don't want to talk—too much. You were all *brilliant* today.

People disperse.

SHE

Oh my God.

HE

What?

SHE

He hates me.

HE

No.

SHE

Thanks. See you tomorrow.

HE

See you tomorrow.

Pause.

SHE

Do you still have my shirt?

HE

Which one?

SHE

The one with the—?

HE

Yes. Do you have mine?

SHE

Maybe. Say hi to the schoolteacher.

HE

Say hi to your husband.

SHE

Will do.

Scene 3—The Next Day

Your leading man is ill today. His understudy will rehearse with you.

Oh. What kind of illness does he have?

Stomach bug.

Oh, really.
Who is his understudy?

Kevin, the understudy, comes on.

Hi.

SHE

(To the director) I thought he was playing the butler.

DIRECTOR

He is. He's also understudying Johnny. And the husband. He was my student when I was teaching Meisner? He's really something.

KEVIN

I didn't get a chance to say: I'm—a fan. A huge fan—that thing you did? Like ten years ago—whoa. That was incredible.

SHE

You saw that? Oh, thanks, you're sweet.

DIRECTOR

Take it from: "Kiss me darling."

KEVIN

What a strange job to kiss strangers in front of people and make it look like you know each other. Or kiss someone you know in front of people and make it look like a stranger.

SHE

Yeah. It is.

KEVIN

Where do you want me?

SHE

Just here.
Whenever you're ready.

KEVIN AS JOHNNY

Kiss me darling.

They kiss. She stops.

SHE

Sorry—

KEVIN

What is it?

SHE

You're making a little face before you kiss me, sort of like you're going to eat me.

KEVIN

I'm sorry. I'm nervous.

SHE

Oh—

KEVIN

Also, I'm not straight.

SHE

Oh?

KEVIN

Yeah. It's not a problem, obviously, I just have this awful fantasy that I'll kiss a woman on stage and everyone will be like: you know, *yeah right*, whatever. Sorry I just needed to get that out there.

SHE

Don't worry. You're going to be great.

KEVIN

Thanks. Cool. Cool.
(As Johnny) Kiss me darling.

They kiss.
He makes a face like he's going to eat her.
She pulls away.

KEVIN

What is it?

SHE

Sorry—just a weird flashback to prom—sorry, nothing.

DIRECTOR

Let's just—okay—maybe it would help to be clinical. From: "Oh, Johnny"—and I think it's a five count kiss—or maybe a three count kiss—if that helps.

SHE AS ADA

Oh, Johnny. Johnny Lowell.

KEVIN AS JOHNNY

Ada . . . I can't and I won't call you by your married name, god-dammit to hell. I never met and never will meet Ada Wilcox. Kiss me again, Ada Fountain. Kiss me back in time.

They kiss.
He makes a face like he's going to eat her first.

DIRECTOR

One—two—three—

SHE

Okay. I think we're good.

Scene 4

More rehearsal furniture has been imported.
A chaise, a potted palm.
The actors are wearing some pieces of costumes now.
Street clothes or jeans, paired with glorious satin tops, hats, gloves.

DIRECTOR

I'd like to just run that straight through without stopping, if we
can manage it.
From the top?

SHE

Right.
(To He) Stomach bug?

HE

Yeah.

SHE

Really?

HE

Yes—my stomach hurt.

SHE

Hmm.

HE

And I made the mistake of listening to *Blood on the Tracks* and smoking a pack of cigarettes.

Their favorite album.

SHE

Oh, God, why'd you do that?

HE

I don't know because I'm a total fucking idiot.

He touches the tassel on her robe and exits.

DIRECTOR

Music . . .
(The director hums) . . . and, the curtain goes up . . . and there you are . . .

She as Ada, lying on a divan.
A maid adjusts her pillow.

MAID

Anything else, mum?

SHE AS ADA

Oh, no, Millicent. Just draw the curtains, if you would.
(As herself) Why is everyone in this play called Millicent?

The maid draws the curtains.

DIRECTOR

(Overlapping) Keep going—

44

SHE AS ADA

Thank you, you're such a dear. Millicent.

MAID

The doctor is here to see you, ma'am.

SHE AS ADA

Send him in.

The husband enters.

HUSBAND

Feeling better after a nap, darling?

SHE AS ADA

I'm clean wiped out.

The doctor enters.
She sits up.

SHE AS ADA

Hello, Doctor.

KEVIN AS DOCTOR

Mrs. Wilcox. Mr. Wilcox. We've done some tests, and . . .

SHE AS ADA

What is it, Doctor?

KEVIN AS DOCTOR

Well, I'm afraid the news is not good.

SHE AS ADA

Tell me straight away, I'm a strong lady. You should see me run
in heels.

She laughs, mordantly.
Everyone looks at her.

SHE

It says, "She laughs, mordantly."

DIRECTOR

I've crossed out all the stage directions.

SHE

Oh.

KEVIN AS DOCTOR

Mrs. Wilcox, I'm afraid you have—Johnson's disease.

SHE AS ADA

Johnson's disease?

KEVIN AS DOCTOR

Johnson's disease.

SHE AS ADA

My disease is named after someone? That's better than having an unnamed disease, isn't it? Ha ha.

She laughs. No one else laughs.

SHE

That was a hollow laugh.

DIRECTOR

Right. Good.

HUSBAND

But what does it mean, Doctor? Will she have to alter her way of life?

KEVIN AS DOCTOR

Mr. Wilcox . . . Mrs. Wilcox . . .

SHE AS ADA

Yes.

KEVIN AS DOCTOR

I don't know how to tell you this . . . you haven't got very much
time.

SHE AS ADA

I have all the time in the world! Haven't I?
(Looking around wildly, to her husband)
Haven't we, darling?

KEVIN AS DOCTOR

I'm afraid not.

SHE AS ADA

Doctor, you've been a friend to our family for years—be a friend
now: Lie to us, then leave. Will I have to alter my way of life?

KEVIN AS DOCTOR

No. It's only that—you should do whatever it is that you would
like to do, for the next month.

SHE AS ADA

The next *month*?

KEVIN AS DOCTOR

That's right.

SHE AS ADA

Am I to die in August?
Why die in August when you could die in the spring? Or a
Christmas death would be economical, all the furs you wouldn't
have to buy for me?

The men look down, solemn.

SHE AS ADA

No one has a sense of humor today, I see. Thank you for coming, Doctor.

KEVIN AS DOCTOR

Thank you. Mrs. Wilcox—take care of yourself.

SHE AS ADA

Why you take care of *yourself*, Doctor, doctors always forget to take care of themselves.

He exits.
She turns to her husband.
She bursts into tears.

HUSBAND

You put a brave face on it, darling.

SHE AS ADA

August? *August?* Why Millie only gets home from Paris in two weeks . . . August?

She sobs on her husband's chest. He watches.

HUSBAND

I will take good care of you, darling, never you fear.

SHE AS ADA

I am not afraid.

HUSBAND

My brave darling.
What can I get you? What can I give you?
Shall we go home—to your parents' house, to Seaberry farm?
The fresh Midwestern air might do you good. What would you like? Anything, anything?
(As himself) Too much?

DIRECTOR

We can calibrate the style after the first preview.
Trust your instincts for now.

HUSBAND

Anything, anything!

SHE AS ADA

No, no, I want to stay here, at home.

HUSBAND

I'll quit my job.

SHE AS ADA

No, no, everything must go on as usual. It must. You must get up every morning, and put on that silly suit and tie and go to work. You must do that for me.

HUSBAND

(In low tones) Then I shall.

A pause.

SHE AS ADA

There's only one thing.

HUSBAND

What is it darling?

SHE AS ADA

I have to—
I have to see Johnny Lowell before I die. *(The husband turns away. And turns back)*
I never said good-bye. We ended things so badly. Will you do that for me? I know how you must hate the sight of him. But I must see him. I must—say good-bye.

HUSBAND

Anything, dear.

SHE AS ADA

Will you cable him?

HUSBAND

Yes.

SHE AS ADA

I believe he's in Sweden. Doing a sculpture—a very large one—I've no idea. But cable him, will you? That's the only thing I ask of you. That—and to behave as though nothing at all is the matter. We won't tell Millie. She shouldn't be thinking of death and disease on her first European tour.

HUSBAND

I can't bear it.

SHE AS ADA

Stiff upper lip, darling. I don't feel so bad. *(She coughs loudly)* *(As herself)* Too much?
(She as Ada, coughs softly) Just a little weak, is all. Let's do all the things we used to do. Let's trip the light fantastic. Remember that old song we used to sing?

They sing; she starts and the husband joins.

SHE AS ADA/HUSBAND

Can we live on love and cereal?
Only in the rain . . .

Is the moon all that ethereal
In Italy or Spain—

Will you come up to my room—
Tie a staircase to the moon—

I suppose it's immaterial
Cuz it's you you you you you . . .

DIRECTOR

Good. Scene Two!

SHE

Notes?

DIRECTOR

I don't think so. No. Not at this point.

SHE

Are you sure? I'd be happy for some guidance.

DIRECTOR

Premature!
I want to press on—for momentum.
The arrival of Johnny Lowell.

The maid enters.

MAID

Madam: Johnny Lowell has arrived.

Johnny Lowell enters.

SHE AS ADA

Is it you?

HE AS JOHNNY

Ada, my God, Ada.

She swoons a little.

HE AS JOHNNY

Ada, you're not well. Lie down.

SHE AS ADA

I'm fine, Johnny, just a little tired is all.

HE AS JOHNNY

Here, on the divan . . .
(As himself, trying a different pronunciation) Divan? Divan.
(As Johnny) I'll lie next to you.

He lies on the divan with her and holds her hand.

HE AS JOHNNY

This is how it was. Exactly how it was. When we were eighteen, and had our lives in front of us . . .

He moves to kiss her.

SHE AS ADA

Johnny, I'm a married woman now . . .

HE AS JOHNNY

You told me to come.

SHE AS ADA

Yes.

HE AS JOHNNY

Death and marriage are nothing to us. You *know* that. Kiss me.

Almost kissing her.

SHE AS ADA

It is as though no time had passed! As though we were still standing on that dock . . . But, Johnny, you must know—
I can't betray him—

HE AS JOHNNY

I always said you would end up with a man with a briefcase.
I knew that, even when we began our doomed romance.

HE

Can we cut the word doomed?

DIRECTOR

I don't think the estate of Erbmann, Landor and Marmel would let us change it. They're very particular. I could hardly get the rights for New Haven.

HE

Isn't a bad sign when three people wrote a play? I mean if two people wrote it, it's one thing, but three, come on, three?

DIRECTOR

Just try it.

HE

Okay.

(As Johnny) I always said you would end up with a man with a briefcase. I knew that, even when we began our doomed romance. But don't tell me you've become conventional, darling—kiss me—one last kiss . . .

That's what I came for, isn't it? One last kiss. You're as beautiful as the day I met you.

SHE AS ADA

Am I?

HE AS JOHNNY

(Very sincerely, dropping out of character, slightly) Yes, only I wish I'd put these lines on your face myself. Each one.

He traces the lines on her face, tenderly.
They kiss.

SHE AS ADA

Oh, Johnny!

HE

Line—

DIRECTOR

"Let me take you to Sweden—"

HE AS JOHNNY

(Overlapping) Let me take you to Sweden. You should die in a place where the trees are higher than the buildings.

SHE AS ADA

No, I prefer to die where the buildings are higher than the trees. I'm a city girl. I like to be perched high above everything—so I can see.

HE AS JOHNNY

Above everything—including people.

SHE AS ADA

What's that supposed to mean?

HE AS JOHNNY

(Talking as both Johnny and He) It was as though you were always perched above me, taking in the view, you couldn't even see my face.

SHE

(Not her line at all) Seriously? I saw your face!
What?
Line?

DIRECTOR

"I can't help it if you aren't very tall."

SHE AS ADA

I can't help it if you aren't very tall.

HE AS JOHNNY

Don't be glib!

SHE AS ADA

I was mad about you! Mad! Don't you see?

HE AS JOHNNY

Then why'd you leave, Ada!

SHE AS ADA

It was impossible! Perhaps if I'd loved you less it would have been hunky-dory!
I loved you too much!

They look at each other.
For longer than is required.

DIRECTOR

"I think I hear my husband."

SHE AS ADA

I think I hear my husband. Hang it all!

Husband enters.

HUSBAND

Hello, Johnny. Welcome to New York. I understand you've been in Sweden?

HE AS JOHNNY

That's right. *(He says something in Swedish)* That means: "Thanks for having me. It's good of you." In Swedish. I'm sorry about the—circumstances.

HUSBAND

Oh, don't mention it, she doesn't want it mentioned.
Do you have everything you need to make you comfortable?

HE AS JOHNNY

Almost everything.

Johnny looks at Ada.

HUSBAND

Well, let me know if there is anything I can do to make your stay more comfortable.

HE AS JOHNNY

I will.

HUSBAND

Would you like a drink?

HE AS JOHNNY

A whiskey sour.

HUSBAND

Ada?

SHE AS ADA

I'm afraid I can't drink cocktails anymore.

HUSBAND

Of course. Sorry, darling.

Husband exits.

HE AS JOHNNY

My God, he spoke to me like a hotel concierge.
The only thing missing was the uniform.
Kiss me.

He pulls her toward him. They kiss.

HE AS JOHNNY

By God, I've missed your lips—

SHE

Wait, maybe more like—

They kiss again, and she drives the kiss.

SHE AS ADA

Your lips taste like—let me taste them again.

She does.

SHE AS ADA

Of cherries?

She tastes them again.

SHE AS ADA

Of chestnuts . . .

They kiss more than is required.
The director gets uncomfortable.

DIRECTOR

"Oh God, I want to kiss you all day . . ."

SHE AS ADA

Oh God, I want to kiss you all day! Until I'm breathless with desire. The way I was when I was eighteen. Do you remember the lake? And Florence, high above the hill?

HE AS JOHNNY

Let me die with you.

SHE AS ADA

No, no.

HE AS JOHNNY

Yes, at the same time.

SHE AS ADA

Darling, we'd both be dead, what's the use?

HE AS JOHNNY

I'll stay with you—until the moment comes. I will be here, keeping hold of your hand.

SHE AS ADA

You won't lose courage?

HE AS JOHNNY

No.

SHE AS ADA

Oh, Johnny.

SHE

Oh that's where I have to cry—oh—

DIRECTOR

Yeah.

HE

You can just do it right here—

He gestures to his torso. She weeps onto his torso.

SHE AS ADA

Oh Johnny!

HE AS JOHNNY

There there. I never could stand it when you cried.

SHE AS ADA

I didn't cry so very much, did I? We were happy, weren't we?

HE AS JOHNNY

No, darling. But it was heaven—being miserable with you.

He strokes her hair.
Enter husband.

HUSBAND

Darling, Millicent telephoned to say that she's on one of these new-fangled diets and doesn't eat—

Johnny keeps stroking her hair.

HUSBAND

Doesn't eat meat. Can you imagine? She's been to India—can you imagine—not—eating—meat?

HE AS JOHNNY

I love a turkey sandwich. A cheese sandwich just doesn't cut it.

Johnny, still stroking her hair.

HUSBAND

You're just going to—stroke my wife's hair in front of me?

HE AS JOHNNY

You did invite me, didn't you? Otherwise, why don't you stroke her hair?

HUSBAND

I'm happy to stroke my wife's hair.

HE AS JOHNNY

Let's both stroke her hair.

SHE AS ADA

Oh, both of you get out of here and play billiards!
(As herself) And then I exit stage left?

DIRECTOR

Why don't you go stage right. Because you have your quick change.

SHE

Right. Are we going to rehearse the quick change before the dress?

DIRECTOR

We can rehearse it now, before the break, if you like.

SHE

That'd be good. Time it.

DIRECTOR

Go!

She exits.
All the actors sit around, behaving like actors.
The contrast between the fake world of their costumes
and the real modern world: phones, Doritos,
sitting, waiting, knitting . . .
She enters.

SHE

How was that?

DIRECTOR

Thirty-two seconds.

SHE

Great!

DIRECTOR

Take ten.

She sits in her gorgeous green dress on the lip of the stage and opens
a water bottle.
They might share a cigarette. If they do, He says:

HE

Do you mind if I smoke?

SHE

No.

HE

Is your husband coming to see the dress?

SHE

God, no. I told him to stay away until opening.

HE

And will you kiss me less passionately in front of him?

SHE

I don't know yet.

HE

What does he do, anyway, your husband?

SHE

Mergers and acquisitions.

HE

Ah.

SHE

My mother told me never to marry an actor. She said never marry a man who looks in the mirror more than you do.

HE

Your mother never liked me.

SHE

Mmm—

HE

But I don't look in the mirror.

SHE

No, you didn't.

HE

I wanted to be ugly. A writer. Make something lasting.

SHE

Were you ever unambivalent—about anything?

HE

You.

SHE

For a time.

HE

For a time.

SHE

Favorite last line from a play:

HE/SHE

I fell in love with James Tyrone and was so happy for a time . . .

A pause.

HE

Are you happy?

SHE

We're happy. My husband, I mean. And me. We're happy.

HE

Good. Good for you.

SHE

My daughter is gorgeous. My daughter is the love of my life.

HE

I'm so happy for you.

SHE

We don't fight. My husband. And I. He's comforting. He comforts me.

HE

Like a hot cup of tea? With exactly the right amount of milk?

SHE

No, more like a person. Who exhibits restraint and compassion.

HE

Like tea. Remember that time in Düsseldorf when we were on tour and I said let's have sex I want you. And you said but I have water on to boil for tea. I knew then that we were finished.

SHE

That's not how it went. I made the tea anyway and then we did it and then I warmed up the tea in the microwave and I drank it after we did it.

HE

Whatever.

SHE

I like tea.

HE

I know.

SHE

It wasn't about you.

HE

Right.

SHE

This play is kind of awful, don't you think?

HE

Oh, I don't know . . . I like your costumes.

SHE

Do you.

HE

Yes, this greenish one is especially fetching. With the little thing done up just here . . .

He touches her shoulder.

SHE

Why, thank you. Johnny Lowell.

HE

Ada Fountain, my darling, how *can* we have been apart for so long?

SHE

(As Ada) I do not know.
(As herself) I don't know.

He moves in to kiss her.
She looks around and moves away.

SHE

Stop!
I love my husband.

HE

You always found repression so interesting. I don't find repression interesting. I really, really want you.

SHE

How's your schoolteacher?

HE

Optimistic.

SHE

I missed you.

HE

A lot?

SHE

A lot.

HE

It's torture kissing you on stage, in front of all these idiots. I want to fling you on a bed, press you against a door—Oh, God, you're killing me.

SHE

Why do you think people enjoy watching other people kiss on stage, anyway?

HE

They don't enjoy it. They tolerate it.

SHE

What do you mean?

HE

They tolerate it because it signifies resolution which people like to see on stage but they don't really like to see the act of kissing on stage, only the idea of kissing on stage. That's why actors have to be good looking because it's about an idea, an idea of beauty completing itself. You don't like to see people do more than kiss on stage, it's repulsive.

SHE

But why do we want to see people have sex in the movies.

Throughout the following he might touch her knee.

HE

That's because you can be alone in your own mind when you watch a movie and it's like masturbation but you can't be alone when you watch a play because there's always someone next to you. That's why it's uncomfortable to watch people have sex on stage but pleasant to watch them have sex in the movies. And that's why porn stars don't have to be as good looking as actors because we're not watching the *idea* of sex but sex itself which can be ugly. And that's why the theater is superior to film, because it's less like masturbation.

DIRECTOR

Places!

They leap apart.
The butler enters with Millicent.

KEVIN AS BUTLER

Millicent Sternhaven.

SHE AS ADA

Hello, Millicent, my darling.

MILLICENT

Ada, dear, how *are you? How are you?*

SHE AS ADA

For God's sake Millicent, don't talk in italics, I'm perfectly fine. News travels fast, doesn't it, bad news faster than good . . .

MILLICENT

Can I get you anything, my dear?

SHE AS ADA

Just get me out of here, if one more person is solicitous, I'll scream. You, of all people, Millicent, can be mean. Be mean to me, that's what I crave more than hot compresses. I command you to be mean.

MILLICENT

I'm not sure I can do it on command, dear. It's part of my charm—I'm mean on impulse.

Enter Johnny Lowell.

SHE AS ADA

This is my old friend Johnny Lowell, just in from Sweden.

MILLICENT

Pleased to meet you. Whatever were you doing in Sweden?

HE AS JOHNNY

I like to make sculptures. Very large sculptures. With my hands, you know.

MILLICENT

Ah!

Millicent looks at his hands.

HE AS JOHNNY

But then Ada cabled me to come at once as she was dying and of course I came straight away.

SHE AS ADA

Don't believe a word he says—
(As herself) Wait—is this the long cross in the blocking you changed last night?

DIRECTOR

Yes. You have to cross stage left because of sightlines.

SHE

Right. So—
(As Ada, to Millicent, over her shoulder as she crosses) Don't believe a word he says—I'm not dying—no one here is dying—at least not today—

Ada crosses the room grandly and trips and falls.

SHE

Uum?

He rushes to help her, trips over a lamp cord or a potted palm, and falls down.

SHE

Are you okay?

HE

Ah! My ankle.

SHE

Oh!

Scene 5—Putting the Understudy in for Previews

SHE

How long does an ankle stay broken?

DIRECTOR

Six weeks or so.

SHE

Fuck!

DIRECTOR

Luckily we have an understudy . . .

SHE

He makes this face—this weird face—like he's going to eat me—before he kisses me—like a placoderm—

DIRECTOR

What?

SHE

You know, one of those jawless prehistoric fish—with teeth?

DIRECTOR

(Overlapping) We don't really have a choice. Opening night is in a week.

SHE

Can't he do it on crutches?

DIRECTOR

I—I don't know how he could—

SHE

(Overlapping) Jesus!

Kevin enters.

SHE

Hello, Kevin.

KEVIN

Hi, hi.

DIRECTOR

So let's start with Scene Three.
You're just here, and you're just here.
"It is as though no time had passed—"

SHE AS ADA

(Flatly) It is as though no time had passed! As though we were still standing on that dock . . . But, Johnny, you must know— I can't betray him—

KEVIN AS JOHNNY

I always said you would end up with a man in a briefcase.

SHE

What?

KEVIN AS JOHNNY

(Overlapping) With a briefcase. I knew that, when we began our doomed romance. But don't tell me you've become conventional, darling—kiss me—one last kiss—that's what I came for, isn't it? One last kiss. You're as beautiful as the day I met you.

SHE AS ADA

Am I?

KEVIN AS JOHNNY

Yes, only I wish I'd put these lines on your face myself. Each one.

He traces the lines on her face. They kiss.

SHE AS ADA

Oh, Johnny!

SHE

Can I just— It's more like . . . Could someone—let me show you. Millicent!

The actress playing Millicent enters.

ACTRESS

Yes?

SHE

I'll be Johnny Lowell, and Millicent, you be me.
(As Johnny) Yes, only I wish I'd put these lines on your face myself. Each one.

She kisses the actress playing Millicent the way Johnny Lowell kissed her.

SHE

(To Kevin) Okay?
(To actress) Thanks.

ACTRESS

No problem.

KEVIN

Okay. Like: *(As Johnny)* I wish I'd put these lines on myself your face.

SHE

What?

KEVIN AS JOHNNY

Each one.

He traces the lines on her face. They kiss, awkwardly.

SHE AS ADA

Oh, Johnny!
(As herself) I'm sorry. I just— I quit.

Scene 6

A marquis might come down. It says in lights:
    The Last Kiss
    By Landor, Erbmann and Marmel
    With a new prologue
    By the director, Adrian Schwalbach

DIRECTOR

(Prerecorded message) Please turn off those cell phones and open those candies! And the New Haven fire department would be much obliged if you would take a look and see where your nearest exit is. There will be one intermission, and I know the lines to the ladies bathrooms are long so please make a beeline. Thank you, relax, we know you have a choice of theaters so we appreciate you choosing us. And now *The Last Kiss* by Landor, Erbmann and Marmel with a new prologue by the director, Adrian Schwalbach.

The sound of sweeping overture music.
Lights up on Johnny, who enters, on crutches.

The butler also enters.
Applause.
A prologue:

HE AS JOHNNY

Give me the telegram, Jenkins.

It says to come at once. My God, Ada . . . my beautiful girl . . . how can it be . . .

How the hell am I going to get from Sweden to New York City on these damn crutches?

With my usual aplomb, I suppose!

I must be the only sculptor to have had a marble head fall on my foot!

Canned laughter from the audience.

HE AS JOHNNY

Jenkins, book me a first-class ticket on the SS *Richmond* at once.

Ada, I'm coming, I'm coming, as fast as I can, wait for me!

He shuffles off slowly on his crutches.

Scene 6.5—The Last Scene of the Play

An opulent, beautiful 1930s set is revealed.
A New York apartment (balcony, chandeliers, columns) glides on.
Johnny Lowell has just told Ada Wilcox that he is eloping to Swe-
den with her daughter. She slaps He.

SHE AS ADA

You're eloping to Sweden with my daughter. Are you trying to
drive me to the brink of insanity?

HE AS JOHNNY

How can you blame me? She's the very picture of you.

SHE AS ADA

You were a cad then and you're a cad now, Johnny Lowell. My
daughter deserves better.

HE AS JOHNNY

Better than this?

Johnny kisses Ada.
She wipes the kiss off on her shirtsleeve.

SHE AS ADA

You're sick.

HE AS JOHNNY

At least admit that I cured your disease . . . one kiss from me, and I sent death packing . . . you're positively blooming again. I know you cannot forgive me. But please, forgive Millie. It's not her fault.

SHE AS ADA

I do not blame Millie. I blame myself. Oh, Johnny. One more song and then we're finished.

They sing a song and do a small dance, which is complicated by his crutches.

HE AS JOHNNY/SHE AS ADA

No one says farewell these days
They all just say good-bye

No one says farewell these days
They hire a car, or fly

If onlys are for fools and lovers
Farewells are for the birds

So good-bye to you my first true love
Good-bye—what a horrible—word—

Johnny exits.

SHE AS ADA

(Alone) Good-bye, Johnny . . .

She sinks down onto the divan.
Her husband enters.

HUSBAND

Darling. I should never have allowed him into our home.

SHE AS ADA

Do not reproach yourself, my dear. I have learned something very important. I used to think that Johnny was the man I was meant to die with, and you were the man I was meant to live with. I now know the truth: the one you are meant to live with is the one you are meant to die with. Darling, it's you—it's you forevermore.

HUSBAND

Oh, darling. Don't speak of death now that we are out of his crutches—clutches . . . You look so healthy, my dear, so robust.

SHE AS ADA

Jack—I love you, as I have never loved you, or anyone else, before . . . Only there is one thing I must tell you.

HUSBAND

What is it?

SHE AS ADA

I'm afraid Johnny did not go alone to Sweden.

HUSBAND

Has he taken up with the parlor maid?

SHE AS ADA

No. He has taken Millie with him.

HUSBAND

Millie? Our daughter? How is this possible? He did not ask my permission—Millie? To Sweden? He must be stopped—I will stop him—I will go—now—Jenkins!—book me a first-class ticket on the SS *Richmond* to Sweden—oh—ah—

The husband has a heart attack.

SHE AS ADA

Jack! Jack! Jack! No! No! Help! Millicent! Jenkins! Someone! Help!
Oh God! Jack!

The husband falls. He is in the throes of dying.
She kisses his face. She holds him, weeping.

SHE AS ADA

Jack—wait for me on the threshold, I will keep hold of your hand . . . The angels are calling you, Jack, saying we have met one of our own . . . a little angel named Jack . . . you are the most good, the most good man—

She sobs and rocks him.
He dies.

SHE AS ADA

Am I to meet life on my own then? Ada Fountain—and life . . . life . . .

Applause.
The company bows.
It might be nice if we saw them bow from the back,
suddenly transported backstage.
The director might watch from backstage, moved.
Johnny Lowell enters and bows with his crutches.
The leading lady bows on her own.
Wild applause for the leading lady.

Scene 7

Backstage. The sound of applause.
He and She backstage. He leans on his crutches.

HE

They liked it.

SHE

They seemed to. How odd.

HE

There's no accounting for taste.
They're still clapping. Should we go on for another bow?

SHE

You whore.

HE

Should we?

SHE

No.
Let's hide.

HE

Let's.

They hide.

HE

I couldn't take my eyes off you, I almost dropped a line, you were
on fire.

SHE

But you didn't.

HE

What?

SHE

Drop a line.

HE

No.

SHE

I wasn't *that* distracting.

HE

I was watching from the wings, your last speech. It was so real.
Even though the language was, I'm sorry, so fucking fake.

SHE

I don't want to go to the party. Let's not go to the party.

HE

Let's not.

SHE

This—here—this feels like my real life. I don't want to be me.
I want to be Ada Wilcox.

HE

I don't want Ada Wilcox.
I want you.

SHE

You do?

HE

Yeah.

They look at each other.
They kiss.
A real kiss.

SHE

I'm scared.

HE

Me too.

SHE

There's no one watching.

HE

That's why I'm scared.

SHE

When I kissed you just now did it feel like an actor kissing an
actor or a person kissing a person because I've kissed you so
many times over the last few weeks I'm starting to not know
the difference.

HE

It felt like a person.

SHE

I'm a person.
I'm scared.

HE

No one will tell us how it will end.

SHE

No one will tell us when to stop.

HE

There may be no end to it . . .

They kiss.
Curtain.

Act Two

Scene 1

*Lights up on a small, cramped, contemporary New York studio
apartment in the East Village.*
A kitchenette, a shower in the kitchen, a toilet.
The contemporary installation of a mess. Hyper-real.
*Ada and Johnny lounging, dressed in full 1930s costume from the
play, looking hungover,*
on a fold-out bed, with a tumbler of whiskey.
A packet of bad reviews is scattered on the floor.

SHE AS ADA
Millicent, would you clear the breakfast things?
Millicent!

Millicent doesn't come.

SHE AS ADA
Honestly, she used to be a reliable girl and now she can't make
a two-egg omelet.

HE AS JOHNNY

Hang breakfast.

He brushes food to the floor.
They kiss.

HE AS JOHNNY

You're as beautiful as the day I met you.

SHE AS ADA

Am I?

HE

Yes.

They kiss.
The sound of the modern city: honks, shouting, a car alarm, a fire engine . . .

SHE

(Yelling out the window) Shut the fuck up!
(To him, indicating the packet of reviews) Did you read these reviews? They hated us.

HE

Yes. They did. Oh, well.

He smells her skin.

HE

For fifteen years I wanted to smell the exact smell of your skin again. Paper, lemon, sweat—God, it's the same smell. It's divine.

They kiss.
They hear rummaging at the door.

SHE

Who could that be.

HE

That'll be Laurie.

SHE

Who's Laurie?

HE

You know—Laurie.

SHE

The schoolteacher?

HE

Yes, her name is Laurie.

SHE

Do you *live together?*

HE

No, no, but she has keys.

SHE

Oh, God.
Does she keep her toothbrush here?
I think I used her toothbrush.
Oh, God.

Laurie, played by Millicent, but now some approximation of a blond, enters.

LAURIE

Hi honey, I brought groceries, I thought you might be out of provisions—oh—hello.

SHE

Hello.

HE

Hey—you met on opening night?

SHE/LAURIE

Yes.

LAURIE

Hi.

SHE

Hi.

LAURIE

You were great. In the play. That one costume! And the whole thing. It was so—neat.

SHE

Thanks. So—where are you from in the Midwest?

LAURIE

How'd you know I'm from the Midwest?

SHE

(Shrugging) Oh, I—

Laurie unpacks groceries—peanut butter, bananas, fruit roll-ups—kid food.

LAURIE

Iowa. Quad Cities? Do you know them?

She shakes her head.

LAURIE

You should visit! My father once said he never met a mean man from Iowa. *(Looking pointedly at He)* So—

HE

(About to say something important) I—

LAURIE

So the show's over?

SHE/HE

Yes.

LAURIE

You must be so relieved. It must have been so exhausting. Night after night . . . all those lines . . .

SHE

Once you know them, it's not really very tiring to repeat them.

LAURIE

Really? I think I would get so tired, repeating the same thing over and over again. That's why I like teaching kindergarten. Every day is different, you never know what to expect! I love children. I can't wait to have children. Of course we haven't been together that long, I don't even know if he likes children? Do you like children?

HE

Of course I like children.
I was a child once.

He takes a swig of whiskey.

LAURIE

Would anyone like some lunch?

SHE

Is it lunchtime?

LAURIE

It's twelve o'clock, isn't it? I never understood how everyone in this city ate so late. Noon comes, and ding I'm starving, it's like, ring the farm bell!

SHE

Ringadingding.

LAURIE

(Not laughing) You're funny.

Laurie starts preparing a meal.

SHE

When people say, you're funny, it makes me feel like they're saying: you're not funny.

LAURIE

Oh no, not at all, I think you're really funny and it's just rare, you know to find a pretty woman who's also funny because usually women are funny to compensate for not being pretty, I find. Or sometimes you meet a pretty and funny woman and find out she used to be like two hundred pounds or got a nose job and you're like: oh, right that's how she developed a sense of humor, in adolescence.
Sandwich?

SHE

No.

HE

No thanks, honey.

She looks at He.

HE

Laurie, I—

LAURIE

(To She) I'm so sorry about the bad reviews. That one seemed really *personal*. But maybe you don't read reviews?

SHE

(To him) Could you *help me*?

HE

My ankle hurts.

SHE

Tell her!

HE

My ankle hurts.

The doorbell rings.

LAURIE

Are you expecting anyone?

HE

No.

He goes to the door.
It's She's husband, Harrison. Played by the husband from Act One.

HE

Uh—Hello?

SHE

Harry! This is my husband—

HARRISON

How did I know you'd be here?

SHE

We came back on the train from New Haven, it was late, too late to—

HARRISON

Take a taxi home?

SHE

Too late to tell you—

HARRISON

Yes?

SHE

That we've—

HARRISON

fallen back in love.

SHE

I'm so sorry.

LAURIE

What?

HE

Laurie, let me explain—

HARRISON

No, let me explain. She always falls in love with whoever she's in a play with. You and—Johnny here—have kissed each other— let's see—nine times a night, eight shows a week, four-week run, two hundred and eighty-eight times. That's not love. That's oxytocin.

LAURIE

You're good at math.

HARRISON

I'm in finance.
Now take off that costume and let's go home.

HE

I'm afraid she can't go home. It wasn't OxyContin—

HARRISON

Oxytocin—

HE

Whatever—I'm afraid it was fate, being cast in that play. We're
in love again.

LAURIE

You are?

HARRISON

Oh, are you?

SHE

I'm sorry, Harrison. I don't mean to be flippant. This is deadly
serious.

SHE/HE

We're in love.

Laurie runs to the bathroom and slams the door.

LAURIE

Asshole!

Angela (She and Harrison's sixteen-year-old daughter) walks in.

ANGELA

(To He) Hi, you're a total asshole.
Mom, come home, you're being a total bitch. Dad's a wreck. He
puked all night. He was like, shivering, on the bathroom floor.

SHE

You were?

HARRISON

Angela, what are you doing here?

SHE

Angela what on earth——? This is my daughter, Angela.

ANGELA

(To He) Nice to meet you, asshole. You sucked in the play.

HE

A pleasure.

ANGELA

I don't mean to be rude, I just didn't think you were very good. And I think my mom is pretty good and I've never understood how good actors could have sex with bad actors, like how could they not know. Actors must be dumb or something because they mismatch all the time. But like I'm a painter and I think it's pretty objective, it's like, can you copy a Renaissance portrait or can't you? You can, great, so you're decent at least, but with acting it's like, you're just doing human behavior so who's to say who's better, but with painters, if they sucked I'd be like, no you can't get with me, don't even try it. You don't see good painters fucking bad painters as much as you see good actors fucking bad actors, and you are fucking right?

SHE

When did you start saying fucking all the time.

ANGELA

When did you start sleeping with the leading man?

Angela looks hard at She and He.
The door of the bathroom flies open and smoke comes out.

SHE

I—

HARRISON

Angela, go home.

Angela glimpses Laurie smoking pot on the toilet.
The bathroom door flies shut.

ANGELA

(To He) So this is your place? It's kind of dumpy. It's kind of dumpy, Mom. I walked up like ten flights of stairs. Do you have any food? I'm starving. Dad forgets to buy groceries when you're gone. And you can't really eat leftover kung pao chicken on an empty stomach unless you're like totally hungover which I'm not.

A toilet flushes.
Laurie comes out, tear-stained and wonky after crying and smoking a joint in the bathroom.

LAURIE

Would you like a sandwich?

ANGELA

Yes!

LAURIE

P b and j?

ANGELA

You rock.

LAURIE

Never underestimate the power of a p b and j to make you feel better. Poor thing. No groceries at home.

SHE

(To Laurie) She has groceries. *(To Harrison)* She has groceries, right?

HARRISON

We have some milk. Look, don't leave me, honey. I can't bear it. I may not be a rakish actor. I might not be a romantic who believes in "fate" or soul mates but I believe in you. I believe in eighteen years of choosing each other, morning after morning.

HE

Not bad.

But she doesn't love you, Harry. Sorry old man.

HARRISON

Would you please stop talking like you're in a 1930s drama.

LAURIE

(To He) Yes, would you please?

(To Harrison) Why don't you believe in soul mates?

HARRISON

I don't believe in God. So I don't believe in soul mates. Some people believe in soul mates but not God. It's an inconsistent position. Super American. Let's go.

LAURIE

Well I believe in God. And soul mates. And I don't think that makes me dumb. Or American.

HE

I don't believe in soul mates.

LAURIE	SHE
You don't?	You don't?

HE

What we think of as the soul is just a mingling of genetics and our parents, in my case, slowly torturing me, or in your case, giving you complete unconditional love.

ANGELA

(About her sandwich) Mm. So good—

LAURIE

You don't believe in souls?

HE

No, not really.

LAURIE

God?

HE

Maybe. Not really.

LAURIE

Jesus! How can you not believe in God!
I'm *moving in* with you how did I not ask you the God question?
I believe in God, goddammit! I believe in God. And souls. And
soul mates. You're just a *sucker* if you don't believe in the invis-
ible world. You're just particulate *matter*. How can you believe
in fate if you don't believe in God? Fuck!

ANGELA

Do you have any more marijuana?

LAURIE

(To He) Are you in love with her?
Are you?

HE

Yes. I am.

LAURIE

(To He) I am *not* having this conversation in public.

HE

You asked me in public—

LAURIE

Oh!

Laurie runs into the bathroom again.

SHE

(To He) She's *moving in* with you?

ANGELA

You're all such assholes. Marriage should be like a tattoo. *You leave it on.* That's the point of marriage and tattoos. There's this new removable tattoo ink it's such bullshit like why get one if you want a removable one that's like the *definition* of a tattoo, it's forever. If you're that much of a fucking coward don't get a fucking tattoo and don't get married. Why'd you even have me, you assholes. I hate you. You can't even figure out if you have souls, Jesus, am I just some fucking flesh in baggy clothes to you? *Where are the grown-ups?*
I'm out of here. I'll just take my sandwich and go.

She takes her sandwich and leaves.

SHE

Angela! I'm sorry—

HARRISON

Let her go.

She runs out and follows Angela.

HARRISON

(To Laurie) Thank you for feeding our daughter.

LAURIE

You're welcome. *(To He)* You really don't believe in souls?

HE

No.

LAURIE

Well that is a deal-breaker. Good-bye.

She comes back in without Angela.
A moment.

HE

I don't believe in souls in general but in particular, I believe in
your soul, and your soul, and your soul . . . I don't know how to
explain it.
It's just a feeling.
Like a song you can't quite remember but it moves you every
time you hear it.

Music, faintly.
He begins singing.

HE

Some enchanted evening, when you find your true love, when
you feel her call you, across a crowded room, then fly to her side

One by one a voice is added to the chorus:

ALL

and make her your own . . .
or all through your life . . .
you may dream all alone . . .
Once you have found her, never let her go . . .
once you have found her, never let her go!!!!!!!!

They sing in perfect harmony.
Through some strange choreography,
He and She are now paired. Laurie and Harrison are now paired.
Laurie and Harrison kiss.

SHE

What?

Blackout.

Scene 2

The next day.
Post-coital squalor.
He and She are still dressed in the same clothes,
eating leftover Chinese take-out.

HE

Let's do it.

SHE

Again?

HE

Again.

SHE

How many times can you do it in two hours?

HE

Let's find out.

SHE

People shouldn't have sex. It's too complicated. People shouldn't be inside each other's bodies, it's weird. Kissing is fine, maybe questionable, but childbirth, sex, they should be outlawed. Friendship is sublime.

HE

We were friends.

SHE

For a millisecond. For two days before we became insane from being inside each other's bodies.

HE

Maybe.

SHE

Two days of hope. Two days of potential.

HE

Two days of wondering what it'd be like to kiss you. Remember? You were so young. I think you still slept with stuffed animals.

SHE

Did I? Oh, well, one in particular—

HE

Were you a virgin? I forget.

SHE

Practically.

HE

Practically, hmm.

SHE

Were you?

HE

Essentially.

SHE

As in—

HE

The others were just—girls—you were—

SHE

A woman who slept with stuffed animals?

HE

Yes.

SHE

Remember that apartment? We didn't have a thing.

HE

You had a mattress, on the floor.

SHE

You had a poster of *Contempt*.

HE

We didn't have any money. We snuck into the second act of plays.
We lived on a burrito a day.

SHE

And hot and sour soup, remember? We would buy a quart of
hot and sour soup and the rice came for free and we'd eat it for
two meals.

HE

I didn't have a credit card.

SHE

You still don't have a credit card.

HE

That's true. Oh, and they garnished my student loans while I was in New Haven. I didn't open my mail.

SHE

What?

HE

Yeah. I was meaning to tell you.

SHE

Oh. Well—that's okay.

HE

You can see someone more clearly when you don't have anything. I can see you clearly, as I've never seen anyone before or since.

They kiss.

SHE

Remember how I worked at Berlitz language school. I taught English. I would say: is this a duck or a pencil? A pencil. I was so lonely. I had such a hunger for life, I wanted to live . . .

HE

And now?

SHE

I just want to breathe. It feels different than wanting to live.

HE

Do what you should have done then.

SHE

What?

HE

Hold me forever. Curl up with me in a ball and shut the rest of the world out forever and come live with me in an attic or basement—who cares—and pretend we're the only people in the universe.

SHE

Hm—

HE

Did you miss me?

SHE

You have no idea.
I saw you in every play you were ever in. I never waited to say hello.

HE

I thought you hated me.

SHE

No. I thought it would be nice to reminisce with you one day but I feel like I'm drowning.

HE

It must be the hot and sour soup.

SHE

Yeah.
Poor Angela. I feel terrible.

HE

She'll be okay. Don't think about her right now. Think about me.

SHE

She's so angry.

HE

Teenagers are angry. It's a stage.

SHE

And Laurie? Staying there? Do you think Angela likes Laurie better than me?

HE

No.

SHE

She probably makes home-cooked meals.

HE

Yeah, she is a good cook.
(She looks at him)
Sorry—it's just—really good meatloaf.

SHE

Right.
This place is a mess.
My husband once said you and I would still be together if you'd been prescribed the correct antidepressants.

HE

Your husband is such a romantic.

SHE

He is. Kind of.
Maybe I just need a shower. Or a change of clothes.

She looks at her dress.

SHE

I didn't bring a change of clothes.

HE

You can wear Laurie's clothes.

SHE

No, thanks.
I'm just going to—take a shower.

HE

Let's take a shower!

SHE

I want to shower alone though.

HE

Fine. Go shower.

She goes to the shower, which might be in the kitchenette.

HE

Have fun!

SHE

I will! Don't go anywhere!

HE

Where would I go?

He sits there. Starts to eat some cold Szechuan noodles.
The doorbell rings. He opens the door.
It's the director.

DIRECTOR

Hi.

HE

Hi.

DIRECTOR

You're not answering your phone.

HE

I know.

DIRECTOR

I was worried about you.

HE

Why?

DIRECTOR

Because you weren't answering your phone.

HE

I've been—busy.

DIRECTOR

I can see that.
I called you five times. For an audition.

HE

Oh. Shoot. Did I miss it?

DIRECTOR

Yes. But we could work something out—

HE

Does it pay?

DIRECTOR

It's Detroit Actor's Theater. I think they pay scale.

HE

Never heard of it.

DIRECTOR

It's DAT for short.

HE

DAT? DAT Theater?

DIRECTOR

Look—it's very reputable. It does honest, sort of edgy, high-octane stuff. Actors from both coasts come to work at DAT because the work is really very honest. No frills. It's really about the work.

HE

Oh.
They pay scale?

DIRECTOR

Yes.

HE

I need money.

She enters, freshly showered, wearing a bathrobe with a towel wrapped around her hair.

DIRECTOR

Oh—

SHE

Hi.

DIRECTOR

I didn't know—

SHE

How could you not know—

DIRECTOR

These things always go directly over my head. It's a blessing, really.

SHE

Do you want some—I think we have some—rice?

DIRECTOR

No thanks. I came about an audition.

SHE

Oh, what is it?

DIRECTOR

Something I wrote myself, actually. My first play. Kind of a gritty, downtown New York kind of a thing. I miss New York in the seventies.

Looking at the apartment.

DIRECTOR

Actually, do you mind if I take a picture of your apartment? Research.

SHE

It's a mess, sorry.

DIRECTOR

No, it's *perfect*!

SHE

What are the roles?

DIRECTOR

(Taking a picture of the apartment with his phone) What? Oh, there's a meaty role for the man, but the woman's role is— smaller and—well—she's a whore—an aging whore—she wants to leave the business and become an ophthalmologist—how comfortable are you with nudity on stage?

SHE

My situation has changed. I need the money.

DIRECTOR

Oh.

HE

We'll only go out of town together. We're a package deal. As of now.

SHE

When are auditions?

DIRECTOR

Two hours ago.

SHE

Oh.

DIRECTOR

We could, I guess we could read some of it here?

HE

Do you have the script?

DIRECTOR

As a matter of fact I do.

SHE

I'm all wet.

DIRECTOR

Use it.

SHE

Okay.

DIRECTOR

(Taking out the script) You'll have to share.
I can be the pimp.
Let's see . . . From: "You taste like a whore"?

HE AS JOHNNY

You taste like a whore.

DIRECTOR

Sorry—Could you try an Irish accent?

HE

Yeah. Uh—regular or northern?

DIRECTOR

Oh. Northern.

HE AS JOHNNY

You taste like a whore.

SHE AS WHORE

What does a whore taste—
(As herself) Sorry, am I Irish?

DIRECTOR

No, uh, try a Brooklyn accent.

SHE AS WHORE

(Brooklyn accent) What does a whore taste like?

HE AS JOHNNY

Like blood. And childhood.

SHE AS WHORE

(Indicating an imaginary knife) What is that?

HE AS JOHNNY

A knife. I'm going to leave my mark on you.

SHE AS WHORE

No! Don't!

HE AS JOHNNY

I'll be gentle.

He pretends to make a mark on her inner thigh.

SHE AS WHORE

Oh! No! . . . wait, don't stop, I like it . . .
(Not acting, whispering to him) I can't do this.

HE

(In a low voice to her) We need the money.

SHE

Right.
(To the director) Sorry, could you just give me a sort of overview
of the play?

DIRECTOR

Sure. So, there's this very charismatic soldier in the IRA who
runs guns from New York to Belfast. You meet in Washing-
ton Square Park watching street musicians and fall in love. He
doesn't realize you're a whore. You don't realize he's in the IRA.
When he realizes you're a prostitute he gets violent with you,
and ends up revealing that he's in the IRA. The two of you plan
to escape together, to move to Dublin and open an eye glasses
clinic for poor children, but when you finally get up the courage to tell your pimp you're leaving, your pimp kills you, and in
the last scene, your lover finds you bloody on the floor, and he's
about to shoot himself in the head, when his comrades burst in
the door and kill him first. And there's this sort of rain of bul-
lets, and then they sing a Catholic hymn over the bodies, and
then a small child enters and removes the glasses off your dead
body and puts them on—and this little boy can finally see, and
then a beam of light comes down, and well, I think it will be
rather devastating. Okay?

SHE

Okay.
So in *this* scene—

DIRECTOR

Just trust your instincts.

SHE AS WHORE

You leaving?

HE AS JOHNNY

You want me to stay.

SHE AS WHORE

Dunno.

HE AS JOHNNY

You look like my sister.

SHE AS WHORE

Yeah?

HE AS JOHNNY

Yeah.

SHE AS WHORE

What's her name?

HE AS JOHNNY

Haven't spoken her name in twelve years.

SHE AS WHORE

You wanna? Say her name?

HE AS JOHNNY

Yeah. It was: Holly.

SHE AS WHORE

What happened to her? Holly?

HE AS JOHNNY

Died.

SHE AS WHORE

Sorry.

HE AS JOHNNY

Yeah. What an angel face she had. Kinda like yours.

SHE AS WHORE

How'd she die? IRA?

HE AS JOHNNY

Stop asking questions. You ask too many fucking questions.

They look at the director.

DIRECTOR

Great. Could we take it just from: "Stop asking questions," and make it a little more visceral? Just go to the end of the page.

HE

Okay.
(As Johnny) Stop asking questions. You ask too many fucking questions.

SHE AS WHORE

Okay.

HE AS JOHNNY

Get on the bed.

SHE AS WHORE

No.

DIRECTOR

Oh—you can skip hitting her. That will all get choreographed.
Then there's a knock at the door.

The director knocks.

HE AS JOHNNY

Is that your pimp?

SHE AS WHORE

I work alone.

HE AS JOHNNY

Your brother?

SHE AS WHORE

I'm an only.

HE AS JOHNNY

Husband?

SHE AS WHORE

I wish. I don't have a husband.

HE AS JOHNNY

Who the fuck is it then?

DIRECTOR AS PIMP

Open the goddamn door!

She screams.

HE AS JOHNNY

Shut up!
I said shut up! Shut up, shut up, shut up!

He covers her mouth and muffles her scream.

HE AS JOHNNY

God, you're beautiful.

He kisses her, roughly.

DIRECTOR

Nice work. Whew. Thank you. It's hard to go to those dark places. I know. I know. But it was really deep work. Really good. And I think we can really do this together, you know, I'll make a safe place for us, I promise, in Detroit.

The music of Detroit.

Scene 3

A tech rehearsal. Detroit.
No set change.
It is, oddly, an exact facsimile of He's apartment from New York.
But now it is a set. Maybe there are curtains above it.
Or a new lighting instrument above it.

She is now wearing a whore outfit and He is wearing an Irish sweater and cap.

DIRECTOR
(Over a microphone) Sorry we're just checking sound levels—bear with me, please.
Can we get a little more light on the couch?

The lights are adjusted as they talk.

SHE
It's a little weird—don't you think?

115

HE

What?

SHE

The set?

HE

Yeah.

SHE

They even got this stain, on the couch.

HE

Jesus.

DIRECTOR

(Over the mike to the lighting designer) Okay the sound is fine can we move on? And can we get some daylight in through the window please? But more melancholy? Like light through the dust in Hell's Kitchen at five o'clock in mid-November? No . . . yes . . . less blue . . .

HE

Want to run lines?

SHE

Sure.

HE AS JOHNNY

So I was a freebie, huh? Charity for a foreigner?

SHE AS WHORE

It wasn't like that.

HE AS JOHNNY

Tell me—do you like whoring? Tell me about your first time.

> SHE AS WHORE

Don't wanna.

> HE AS JOHNNY

Tell me.

> SHE AS WHORE

Why?

> HE AS JOHNNY

It hurts me to hear and I want to hurt.

> SHE AS WHORE

The first time I kept my eyes closed. He was as old as my dad. After the first time they all just blurred together. Can't tell 'em apart. I have blurry vision, you know? I told my mom I needed glasses in first grade, she didn't believe me. But I think I like looking at life blurry, you know? Makes things easier. In the morning, before I put my glasses on—that's my favorite part of the day—all blurry.

He moves in to kiss her, as Johnny.

> HE AS JOHNNY

Can you see me? How about this close?

> SHE AS WHORE

All blurry.

> HE AS JOHNNY

I can see you. I can see you just fine. And you look nice—real nice. For a whore.

They kiss.
He pulls her head back by her hair and gazes at her, as called for in the stage directions.

SHE

Okay, okay, I got it.
Remember that time you called me a whore?

HE

You mean in real life?

SHE

Yeah.

HE

Not really.

SHE

You don't?

HE

Oh, wait—right, the time you were sort of acting like a whore?

SHE

I was twenty-four—I needed some independence—I was on *tour*—

HE

You don't cheat on someone you love and tell them on Thanksgiving.

SHE

Sorry. You don't call someone a whore and throw a large electric fan at them.

HE

It was at a bookcase.

SHE

The bookcase was in my direction.

                    HE

Sorry.

                    SHE

It scared me for a long time.

                    HE

Sorry. I really am.

                    SHE

Thanks.

                    DIRECTOR

Okay. Can we jump ahead to the entrance of the pimp?

Kevin enters in a pimp costume.

                    KEVIN AS PIMP

Open the goddamn door!

She screams, as the whore.

                    KEVIN AS PIMP

What are you doing to my lady?

                    HE AS JOHNNY

Sorry—I—this your lady?

                    KEVIN AS PIMP

Yeah.

                    HE AS JOHNNY

I'll leave you two alone then.
See you around, Holly.
And I'm sorry about your blurry vision.
I really am.
You've got nice eyes. Real nice.

DIRECTOR

Okay. Good. Can we tech the shooting bit really quick?

SHE

Sure.

DIRECTOR

Is your blood pack handy?

SHE

Yeah.

DIRECTOR

So from: "You take one step towards that door and I'll—"

KEVIN AS PIMP

You take one step towards that door and I'll—

SHE AS WHORE

What?

The pimp shoots her.
She falls down as if dead.
The blood pack doesn't explode.

DIRECTOR

(Toward a sound designer offstage) The sound of the gunfire was totally off. And why didn't the blood pack go off??? Again? Everyone ready?

The pimp shoots her.
A different gun sound cue.
The blood pack doesn't explode.

DIRECTOR

Hey, can we get a new blood pack after the dinner break? And can we get a sound of a pistol instead of a rifle? Thanks. Okay. Let's take dinner.

People start to clear the stage. He approaches the director.

> **HE**

(To director) Hey, I was thinking, what if I move to exit on "See you around, Holly," then I come back to her and do the line, and then exit on "Real nice"?

> **DIRECTOR**

You know I'm open. Try it.

He tries it with blocking.

> **HE AS JOHNNY**

I'll leave you two alone then.
See you around, Holly.

He moves to exit. Turns back.
Gives her a rough kiss.

> **HE AS JOHNNY**

And I'm sorry about your blurry vision.
I really am.
You've got nice eyes.

He moves to exit. Turns back.

> **HE AS JOHNNY**

Real nice.

She rolls her eyes.

> **DIRECTOR**

Good. Good.

> **HE**

(To She) What?

SHE

Nothing. Also, can we choreograph the kiss, because it's a little rough, and I think I'm bleeding because he bit my upper lip.

DIRECTOR

Do the two of you want to work it out on your own on the dinner break?

SHE

No, I'd prefer it if the director directed it.

DIRECTOR

Okay, so let me get in a little closer to see what you're doing. From "I'll leave you two alone then"?

HE AS JOHNNY

I'll leave you two alone then.
See you around, Holly.

He moves to exit. Turns back.
Gives her a rough kiss.

SHE

Ow.

DIRECTOR

So maybe a little less tongue and teeth? Maybe you sort of swoop in like this? Kevin? *(He demonstrates on Kevin)* So you can see? And sort of bend her back a little, so we don't really see the kiss? *(To Kevin)* Thank you.

KEVIN

You're welcome. No problem.

DIRECTOR

Or: what if you sort of shake her before the kiss, sort of like this?

HE

Okay.

He shakes her.

DIRECTOR

Are you good with that? Was that safe?

SHE

Maybe he could shake me more like this. So my neck isn't involved.

She shakes him.

HE

Ow.

DIRECTOR

You okay?

HE

Sure. How 'bout like this?

He shakes her.

SHE

Jesus.

KEVIN

I actually trained in stage combat?

DIRECTOR

You did?

KEVIN

I mean I'm not like a certified fight choreographer but I'm an advanced actor combatant.

DIRECTOR

Oh I didn't realize, oh that's wonderful. Kevin, could you come take a look at this?

KEVIN

Sure. I would actually shake her more like this?

Kevin shakes her.

KEVIN

Like put your hand here, and then, like this?

Kevin shakes her.

DIRECTOR

Sorry—I'm having trouble seeing—what is it you're doing with her neck?

Kevin demonstrates on the director.

KEVIN

It would be like this, and then this, and like that . . . see . . .

DIRECTOR

Oh, right.
So like this?

The director shakes her again.

KEVIN

But support her neck like this while you're shaking her? That's safer. And *(To She)* really relax your neck, just go jelly. Like this.

The director shakes her.

SHE

Oh—fuck. My neck.

Scene 4

On stage again, but opening night.
He and She on stage in costume.
She wears a removable neck brace.
Kevin enters.

OVER THE INTERCOM

Happy opening night, everyone. This is your half hour. For our leading man and leading lady this is fight call, fight call please.

KEVIN

Happy opening! Do you guys need me for fight call?

SHE

No thanks—

HE

(Overlapping) Thanks, Kevin, I think we have it.

KEVIN

Okay, great. Just be sure you run the fight choreography like three times at half speed—

SHE

Three times?

KEVIN

The American Society for Fight Directors recommends three times—

SHE

Okay. Okay.

KEVIN

Just holler if you need me.

SHE

Thanks, Kevin.

Kevin exits. He and She start going through their first choreographed fight.

HE

Okay do you want to do the last scene first?

SHE

Sure.

HE AS JOHNNY

Get on the bed!

SHE AS WHORE

No.

HE AS JOHNNY

Get on the bed, goddammit!

They go through the fight.

SHE/HE

(Some combination of) Yes and grab and one two three . . .

SHE

Again?

They begin again and go through their fight choreography through the following:

HE AS JOHNNY

Get on the bed!

SHE AS WHORE

No.

HE

That okay?

SHE

Yeah.
I want to go home.

HE

Why? We're here, we have each other.

SHE

I miss my daughter.

HE

You miss her insults?

SHE

Being insulted by your child and loving them anyway is the human condition. You wouldn't understand. You don't have children.

HE

Right, right, I wouldn't understand family life, your refrain, you should set it to music.

SHE

Mmm . . . Sorry can we just do the grab again—
And no— You don't understand the human condition—

HE

(Italics refer to the fight choreography) That is such bullshit—
like this?—I don't understand the human condition because I'm
not a breeder—*kick*—that's so pompous, as though only those
that breed understand—life—*5, 6, 7, 8*—sorry does that hurt—

SHE

No— Men are essentially poking around the margins of exis-
tence— Unless you've given birth—

HE

Breeding, breeding. You're obsessed with breeding.

SHE

You've lived like a child for the last twenty years.

HE

Are you going to crawl?

SHE

You don't understand how a marriage works—how you sacrifice
momentary pleasure for long-term satisfaction—

HE

Right—those of us that don't breed are trivial—why do you
keep blaming me for not having children. I never had children
because I wanted to have them with you, and you broke my
heart, you little bitch.

A silence. They stop doing fight call.

SHE

You say something nice and then you call me a little bitch.
What am I supposed to say.

HE

Say that I'm trivial. Say that I don't matter because I never passed my genes on.

SHE

You're not trivial, you have arrested development. You're like a seventeen year old in man pants. Peter Pan is great in a book—but in real life, people who don't grow up, they're a fucking nightmare.

HE

So I'm a fucking nightmare.

SHE

I didn't say that.

HE

(Overlapping) You said I was a fucking nightmare.

SHE

I just said that if Peter Pan were in real life he would be a fucking nightmare—

HE

So I'm a fucking nightmare. Say what you mean.

SHE

I want to go home.

HE

You want your comfortable routine, you want a station wagon, you've always wanted a station wagon. I don't want a fucking station wagon, I'd rather be dead.

SHE

Why do you always make things black and white? You can own a station wagon and have an interesting life. You can drive a station wagon to a museum. Or a theater. It's nice to have a station wagon, if you could afford to own a car at all, at your age.

HE

Fuck you.

SHE

Oh and you could use some work at the end of Scene One. That false exit—that whole— *(She imitates him in the play)* thing you do? "Sorry about your blurry vision"? Fake. Really fake. No one does false exits in real life. That's why they call them false.

HE

People do false exits all the time in life.

SHE

No they don't!

HE

Yes they do! They can't say the really important thing until they're halfway out the door! That's how it is! As soon as you leave someone you can finally say something halfway true!

SHE

No, people leave. They leave and they change their numbers. They leave in terrible silence. They leave you.

HE

That's what you did to me.
Why? Not a fucking word. Why?

SHE

I was scared of you.

HE

Why?

SHE

Sometimes you were scary. You went through my wallet, my phone calls, my journal— Do you remember the night we both stayed up all night—in a youth hostel?—because we were afraid we would kill each other?

130

HE

Vividly. What was that fight about?

SHE

I can't remember.

There's this Japanese story—about a woman who loved this man, her soul mate, from childhood. Her parents made her marry a farmer instead. She ran off anyway with her soul mate and had kids with him. Years later, she comes back to her family and says: "I'm sorry I ran away." And they say: "What? You've been here the whole time, you've been ill, in bed." And she meets this other version of herself, this ghost, and she embraces this woman, and they become *one person.* And it's this parable, like: which one is the ghost?

Ever since I left you I thought that in some parallel ghost world we had kids we rowed by a canal . . . I thought part of me would be a ghost forever, without you. I was no longer real even when I was happy. I was no longer real especially when I was happy. But no, all along in real time you've gone on being you and I've gone on being me and yes I really love you enough to be ghosted by you my entire life but *my God I left you for a reason.*

They look at each other.
The director enters.

DIRECTOR

Is there a problem?

HE	SHE
No.	Yes.

DIRECTOR

We need you backstage! They want to open the house. We're at places!

Scene 5

The director enters.

DIRECTOR

Hello, everyone. It's a DAT tradition to do a curtain speech before opening night, so here I am. I'm Adrian Schwalbach, the director, and in this case the playwright, thank you. It's so good to be back at DAT Theater after a long hiatus in New York. Welcome to the Midwest premiere of *I loved you before I killed you, or: Blurry.* There will be a party across the street afterwards. Cell phones—off. Fire exits—there—and let's see, what am I forgetting? There will be strobe lights, and gunshots, for those of you who have seizures. Enjoy the show.

Lights up.

HE AS JOHNNY

You look like my sister.

SHE AS WHORE

Yeah?

HE AS JOHNNY

Yeah.

SHE AS WHORE

What's her name?

HE AS JOHNNY

Haven't spoken her name in twelve years.

SHE AS WHORE

You wanna? Say her name?

HE AS JOHNNY

Yeah. It was: Holly.

SHE AS WHORE

What happened to her? Holly?

HE AS JOHNNY

Died.

SHE AS WHORE

Sorry.

HE AS JOHNNY

Yeah. What an angel face she had. Kinda like yours.

SHE AS WHORE

How'd she die? IRA?

HE AS JOHNNY

Stop asking questions. You ask too many fucking questions.

SHE AS WHORE

Okay.

HE AS JOHNNY

Get on the bed.

She looks out at the audience.
She is suddenly a million miles away.
A long pause.

HE AS JOHNNY

Get on the bed, goddammit!
(Under his breath to her) Are you okay?

He tries to do their fight choreography.
She does not do the fight choreography.

KEVIN AS PIMP

(Offstage) Open up in there! Open up goddammit!

HE AS JOHNNY

(Waiting for a response from her and not getting one) Is that your
pimp?

SHE AS WHORE

I work alone.

HE AS JOHNNY

Your brother?

SHE AS WHORE

I'm an only.

HE AS JOHNNY

Husband?

SHE

(As herself) I wish. I miss my husband.

HE

(As himself) You do?

SHE

Yeah.

A reckoning.

HE

(Whispering) Line.

DIRECTOR

(From backstage) "Who the fuck is it then?"

HE AS JOHNNY

Who the fuck is it then?

KEVIN AS PIMP

(Offstage) Open the goddamn door!

HE

Scream goddammit!

She screams a strange little scream.

HE AS JOHNNY

Now shut up!

DIRECTOR

(From backstage) Go on, go on—

KEVIN

It's not my cue!

DIRECTOR

Go.

The director shoves Kevin on stage.
Kevin bursts in wearing a pimp outfit.

KEVIN AS PIMP

What are you doing to my lady?

HE AS JOHNNY

Sorry—I—this your lady?

KEVIN AS PIMP

Yeah.

He doesn't do his fake exit.
He leaves while talking, angry:

HE AS JOHNNY

I'll leave you two alone then.
See you around, Holly.
And I'm sorry about your blurry vision.
I really am.
You've got nice eyes. Real nice.

KEVIN AS PIMP

Who's he?

SHE

My first love.

KEVIN AS PIMP

Oh you love him, do you?

SHE

Yes. And I'm leaving the business.

KEVIN AS PIMP

Over my dead body.
You take one step towards that door and I'll—

She exits.
The pimp shoots at her.
She was supposed to fall down dead but she just exits.
The pimp looks confused.

KEVIN AS PIMP

Okay, then.

He pretends to shoot himself.
Confused applause.

Scene 6

A big empty theater space.
It would be nice if this were the actual back wall
and raw space of whatever theater we are now in,
providing that the space has a bit of poetry to it.

She collapses into a chair.
She takes off her whore makeup in front of a mirror.
He grabs She by the shoulders.

HE

Hey. You broke a cardinal rule.
You never fuck with another actor on stage. I don't care what you do to me offstage, but don't you ever fucking do that again.

SHE

I'm sorry. I didn't mean to.

HE

You didn't mean to? Did you *mean not to?*

SHE

I thought I saw my daughter in the third row.

HE

What?

SHE

I thought I saw my daughter, watching me. In my whore getup. And then I thought I must be hallucinating. And I forgot my lines, my blocking, where I was. And then I starting thinking about the *Wizard of Oz* and Judy Garland and shoes and why shoes bring people home and I was trying to remember what Dorothy said when she clicked her heels together and then I could hear you and you were saying "Get on the bed" and so I got on the bed. I'm sorry.

HE

Jesus.

Harrison and Angela enter.

SHE

Angela! Harry! My God what are you doing here?

HARRISON

I never miss an opening.

SHE

I thought you hated me.

ANGELA

I kind of do.
(To He) You were better in this one, asshole.

HE

Thanks. See ya.

He exits.

SHE

(To Angela) What's on your arm?

ANGELA

A tattoo.
I got a tattoo.

SHE

(Reading it) "Om"?

ANGELA

Yeah. Maybe if you come back home I'll add an "M" and make
it "Mom."

SHE

Angie.

She hugs Angela.
Harrison clears his throat.

HARRISON

Angela, give your mother and me some private time, please.

ANGELA

Where am I supposed to go?

HARRISON

Go somewhere. Get some food.

Harrison gives her money.

SHE

There's a vending machine in the green room.

ANGELA

Will I run into your asshole boyfriend there?

SHE

He's not my boyfriend.

ANGELA

What is he then?

SHE

My scene partner.

ANGELA

Really.

She nods.

ANGELA

Okay.

Angela exits.
She and Harrison look at each other for a long moment.

HARRISON

There's something I need to tell you, darling.

SHE

What is it? No one's sick, are they? What?

HARRISON

I financed this production.

SHE

What?

HARRISON

I commissioned Adrian Schwalbach to write a play about a whore
and an asshole and cast the two of you in it.

SHE

What?
For revenge?

HARRISON

Yes.
<u>And</u>. To wake you up.

She looks at him, curious.

HARRISON

Marriage is about repetition. Every night the sun goes down and the moon comes up and you have another chance to be good. Romance is not about repetition.

SHE

No, it's not.
Harry, I was—

HARRISON

What?

SHE

Well, I was—

HARRISON

Wrong?

SHE

Yes.
I'm sorry.

HARRISON

Thank you.

SHE

But what about Laurie? Nice Laurie? I thought you were in love or something.

HARRISON

Turns out no one's that nice. She's one of the most cruel, passive-aggressive people I ever met. She's not really from Iowa. She's from Illinois. Anyway. Let's go.

142

SHE

Where?

HARRISON

Home.

SHE

Really?
Oh God! Harry! I thought you'd never have me back!

HARRISON

I want you back on one condition.

SHE

Anything.

HARRISON

Teach me how to act.

SHE

What?

HARRISON

I want you to take me to a theater and kiss me once a week, and
pretend I'm someone else.
Once a week I can be whoever you want me to be, and you can
be whoever I want you to be. Kiss me in a place with no history,
and no furniture.

SHE

Okay. I can do that.

HARRISON

Remember when we got married and on the way to the wedding
we stopped off and got water on a mountain somewhere and this
old man behind the counter said, ah you're getting married, and
we said yes, and he said, I wish you every blessing—

SHE

—I wish that you love each other a lot, but not too much, not too much right away, but slowly, over time, so it doesn't explode, like a star.

HARRISON

Yeah.
I always planned to love you over time. I always planned to have forbearance in the face of your inevitable indiscretions.

SHE

Why inevitable?

HARRISON

You have an exquisitely overactive imagination. It wasn't fair to put you in that kissing play and have you speak those lines to that man. It was like giving bacon to a hungry vegetarian.

SHE

Why are you so good to me? Why do you love me still?

HARRISON

Because you bore my only child. Because of your eyes. Because you tolerate my penchant for order. Because after our first kiss I told you I'd love you forever, and God knows why, but I meant what I said.

He enters.
They don't see him, they are so absorbed in each other.

SHE

Oh, my husband.
How did you ever become a banker. You're more like a poet.

HARRISON

I'm good with numbers.

A silence.
Harrison touches her face.
They almost kiss.

HE

Sorry to interrupt.
That was intimate. That was nice. I envy you.
I spoke with your daughter.
She misses you.
You two made a lovely thing.
I'm here to do a non-false exit.

SHE

What?

HE

A good-bye. A real one.

He goes to her. He kisses her on the hair, gently.

HE

Sorry.

SHE

Sorry.

A silence.

HE

Good-bye.

SHE

Good-bye.

He exits and does not look back.
A glorious man, a grown-up man.
They watch him go.

145

SHE

(To her husband) Hello.

HARRISON

Hello.

He pokes his head back in.

HE

How was that?

SHE

It was good.

HE

So: the end?

SHE

The end.

HE

The end.

They nod at each other.
He turns to go.
She and Harrison turn toward each other.
They inch toward one another, like plants to the light.
They kiss. A kiss that is as simple as it is real.
The lights go out.
The end.

Acknowledgments

"I don't mind hiding in a bedroom but hiding in a library seems kind of dry," on page 26, is a quote from *No Time for Comedy* by S. N. Behrman. Thanks to the Rodgers & Hammerstein estate for permission to use a quote from "Some Enchanted Evening." Much gratitude to all the divine and generous actors who helped me work on this play in living rooms, rehearsal halls and theaters, in alphabetical order: Todd Almond, Clea Alsip, Jenny Bacon, David Aaron Baker, Bob Balaban, Alec Baldwin, Jeffrey Carlson, Michael Cerveris, Michael Chernuss, Michael Cyril Creighton, Erica Elam, Dominic Fumusa, Emma Galvin, Jessica Hecht, Scott Jaeck, Danny Jenkins, Patrick Kerr, Ross Lehman, Cristin Milioti, Mark Montgomery, Mary-Louise Parker, Bray Poor and Sarah Tolan-Mee. Much gratitude to Bob Falls, Tim Sanford, Stuart Thompson, Adam Greenfield, André Bishop, Daniel Swee, Alaine Alldaffer, Bruce Ostler and Tanya Palmer. Love and thanks to Jessica Thebus and Rebecca Taichman. Thanks to the McCarter Theatre for having me to the Palmer House where I wrote much of Act One. Thank you dear Tony, Anna, Hope and William. This play is a love note to actors and, as such, I must thank my mother, who took me to the theater when I was a child and made me fall in love with it. "You're a better man than I am, Gunga Din."

COURTESY OF THE JOHN D. AND
CATHERINE T. MACARTHUR FOUNDATION

SARAH RUHL's plays include *The Oldest Boy*, *In the Next Room or the vibrator play* (Pulitzer Prize finalist, Tony Award nominee, Best Play); *The Clean House* (Pulitzer Prize finalist, Susan Smith Blackburn Prize); *Passion Play, a cycle* (Pen American Award, The Fourth Freedom Forum Playwriting Award from The Kennedy Center); *Dead Man's Cell Phone* (Helen Hayes Award); *Melancholy Play*; *Eurydice*; *Orlando*; *Demeter in the City* (NAACP nomination); *Late: a cowboy song* and *Dear Elizabeth*. Her plays have been produced on Broadway at the Lyceum Theatre by Lincoln Center; Off-Broadway at Playwrights Horizons, Second Stage and Lincoln Center's Mitzi Newhouse Theater. They have also been produced across the country, often premiering at Yale Repertory Theatre, Berkeley Repertory Theatre and the Goodman. Originally from Chicago, Ms. Ruhl received her MFA from Brown University where she studied with Paula Vogel. In 2003, she was the recipient of the Helen Merrill Emerging Playwrights Award and the Whiting Writers' Award. She was a member of 13P and of New Dramatists and was awarded the MacArthur Fellowship in 2006. Her book of essays *100 Essays I Don't Have Time to Write* (Faber and Faber) was published this fall. You can read more about her work on www.SarahRuhlplaywright.com. She teaches playwriting at the Yale School of Drama, and she lives in Brooklyn with her family.